C000015710

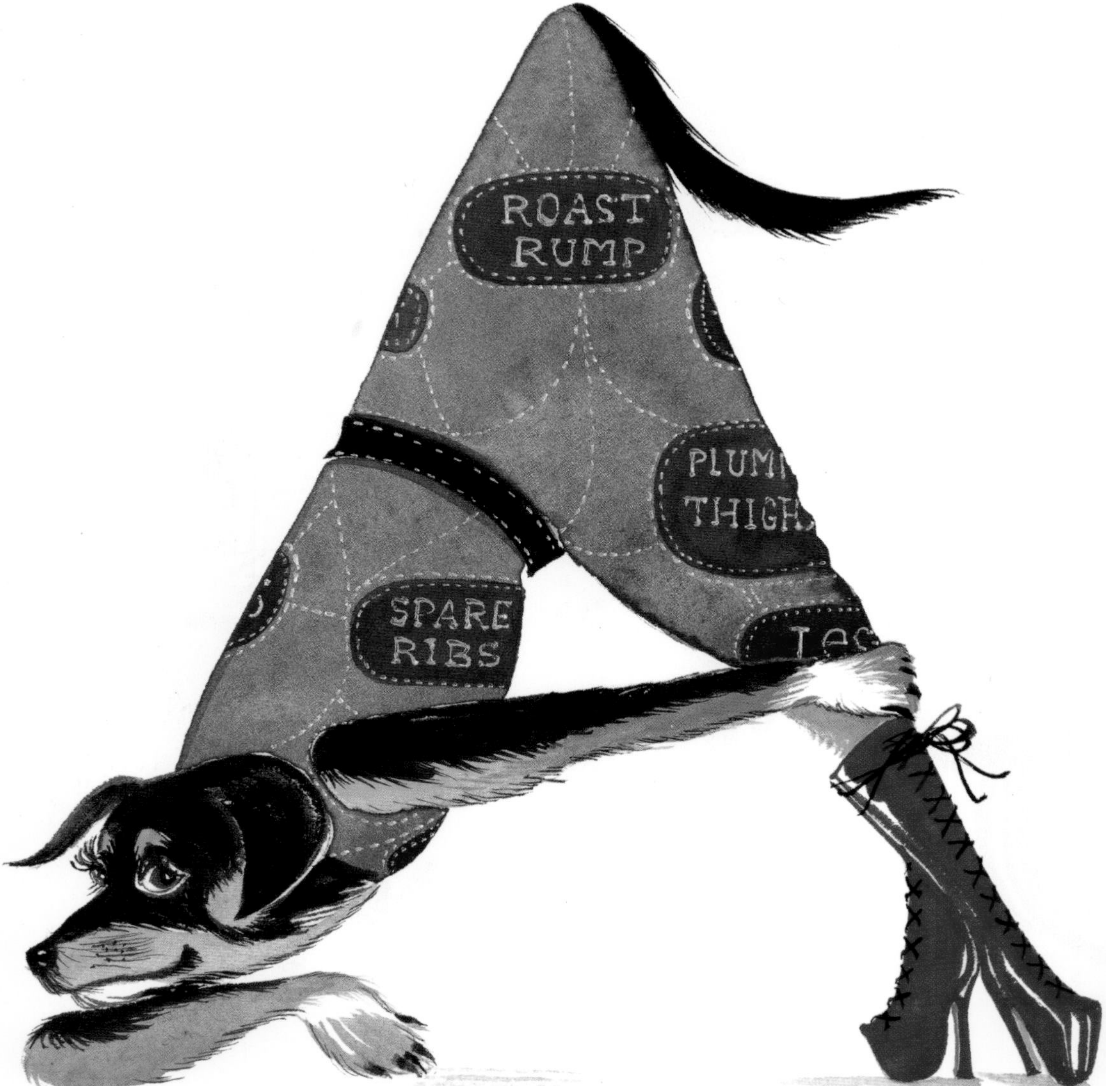
ROAST RUMP
SPARE RIBS

A *is for* Aphrodisiac

" Nothing drives a guy wild with desire like a girl with some meat on her bones. "

A is also for Afro,
because big hair is the perfect place to stash stolen steaks.

B *is for* Biceps

A pumped up red setter called Tim,
Who spent hour after hour at the gym,
Went to terrible pains
To show he had brains
And not just exceptional limbs.

To prove he was more than a cutie
He wore specs and began to talk snooty.
But until he undressed
Girls couldn't care less—
It's a terrible curse being a beauty.

C *is for* Chastity

" It's better to be chaste
and caught than never to
be chaste at all. "

C is also for Complimentary Cold Cuts,
because the sign of true love is free meat.

D *is for* Diaphanous

" When all else fails wear veils. "

D is also for Dominatrix,
because someone has
to teach a dog to sit and beg.

E *is for* Emeralds

" If your romance hits the rocks,
keep the gems and
change the locks. "

F

is for Fat

" Hold onto a man's affections by giving him something to hold onto. "

F is also for **French Poodles,** the natural born enemies of mutts.

G is for Gold Digger

There once was a Yorkie named Busty,
Who wore short skirts and always looked lusty.
She snagged a filthy rich terrier
With a saggy old derriere
And then ran off with the pool boy called Rusty.

(Anonymutt)

H *is for* Highland Fling

“ Never say no to a Scottie in a skirt. ”

H is also for Head over Heels,
a state that is induced by a happy heart and a slippery floor.

I *is for* Me

Lovers swoon under moonlit skies;
Some find love with special guys.
But when I gaze into your eyes
All I see is me.

I is me and me is I.
Who needs thee when I have I?
I'm the apple of my own eye—
This love was meant to be.

Has there ever been such poetry
As the way I feel when I look at me?
Forgive my own immodesty,
But I'm in love with me.

J *is for the* Jugular

" Don't become a jealous wreck.
Sharpen your fangs
and go for the neck. "

J is also for J'Adore,
because love always sounds better in French.

K *is for* Kabob

" Nothing says 'I love you'
like meat on a stick. "

K is also for **Kissing up to the butcher,**
because love dies, but a side of beef lasts forever.

L *is for* Lewd & Lascivious

" Always accept an indecent proposal.

It's better than none at all. "

L is also for Love at first sight,
because the moment I saw a rack of lamb I knew we were meant for each other.

M _is for_ Monogamy

While the dog in me
likes monogamy,
the girl in me wants to roam.
But since girls who date double
tend to get in big trouble,
I'll leave your husband alone.

(Monogamutt)

M is also for Mistress.
Never play second fiddle when you can be the conductor.

N *is for* Nude

"Never wear anything but the fur coat you were born in."

N is also for Neutered. Ouch!

O is for Ogle

" Always give come hither glances
to Old English sheepdogs
with Old English mansions. "

O is also for Orgy,
because two's company
but seven's a party.

P *is for* Pretty

" It's not easy being pretty,

and it's not pretty being easy. "

P is also for Plenty more fish in the sea,
even if you have to trawl the bottom of the ocean to find them.

Q *is for* Quip

" When things get heavy, make light. "

Q is also for Quadriceps,
because you should always make eyes
at guys with great thighs.

R *is for* Riff Raff

I once knew a mongrel called Max
From the wrong side of the tracks.
He was covered in fleas
and a terrible tease
but girls always called him back.

You see, purebreds might be go-getters
Who follow the law to the letter,
But it's dogs from bad homes
who break locks and steal bones
that ladies always like better.

R is also for Retrievers, because someone has to bring my ball back.

S *is for* Snack

" On the menu of love,

not all men are main courses. "

S is also for **Settling down with Sausage dogs,**
because better the dachshund you know than the Doberman you don't.

T *is for* Taxidermy

" When love dies, get it stuffed. "

U is for Undies

A fetching young bulldog named Tess,
With nice lips, and big hips but no chest,
Tried all kinds of ploys
To reel in the boys
Including removing her dress.

But the lads were not to be hooked,
In her direction they never once looked,
Until a push up bra
Turned her into a star
And now she's totally booked.

V *is for* Vodka

" If the eyes of love have trouble seeing, order another drink. "

V is also for Variety,
because when you tire of a chow
there's always a Chihuahua.

W

is for Wag

"Cute tails catch males."

W is also for Wiggle,
because it don't mean a thing if ain't got that swing.

X *is for* Xotic

They say I have Pekingese knees
And the snout of a fluffy Maltese,
With a Labrador's tail
And a Corgi's toe nails,
I'm the child of all family trees.

True, my heritage might be cloudy,
And my parentage no doubt rowdy,
But with a Saint Bernard's chest
And a Norwich's zest,
I'm anything but dowdy.

Y

is for Yacht

" The measure of true love
is about 150 feet. "

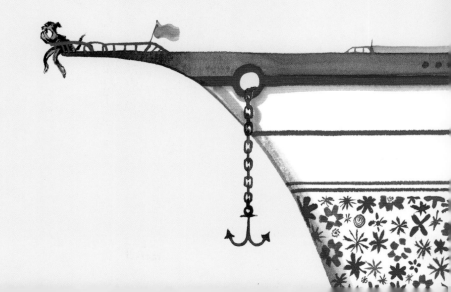

Z

is for Ze End

" Now that I've done my ABC's,

It's time for me to catch some z's.

So if you will excuse me please,

I'm going to bed with my

main squeeze. "